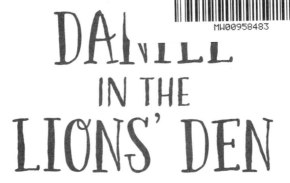

DANIEL
IN THE
LIONS' DEN

BY CHRISTIN DITCHFIELD
ILLUSTRATED BY LEANDRA LA ROSA

A GOLDEN BOOK • NEW YORK

Text copyright © 2022 by Penguin Random House LLC
Cover art and interior illustrations copyright © 2022 by Leandra La Rosa
All rights reserved. Published in the United States by Golden Books, an imprint of Random House
Children's Books, a division of Penguin Random House LLC, 1745 Broadway, New York,
NY 10019. Golden Books, A Golden Book, A Little Golden Book, the G colophon,
and the distinctive gold spine are registered trademarks of Penguin Random House LLC.
rhcbooks.com
Educators and librarians, for a variety of teaching tools, visit us at RHTeachersLibrarians.com
Library of Congress Control Number: 2020934946
ISBN 978-1-9848-9517-2 (trade) — ISBN 978-1-9848-9518-9 (ebook)
Printed in the United States of America
10 9 8 7 6 5 4 3 2 1

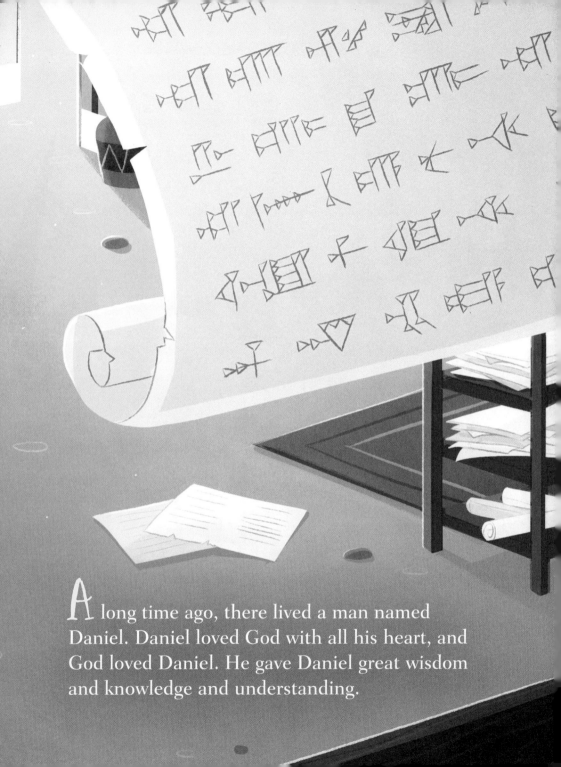

A long time ago, there lived a man named Daniel. Daniel loved God with all his heart, and God loved Daniel. He gave Daniel great wisdom and knowledge and understanding.

Whenever anyone had a problem, Daniel had the answer. Even King Darius, the ruler of Babylon, went to him for advice. Daniel was so helpful that he became the king's closest friend and advisor.

King Darius decided to ask Daniel to help him rule the whole kingdom. This made the king's other advisors jealous, so they tried to find a way to get rid of Daniel.

At first they thought they could catch him doing something wrong, but it seemed Daniel always did what was right.

The advisors came up with another plan. They suggested to the king that he create a new law: for thirty days, no one could pray to anyone but him.

The advisors knew how much Daniel loved to pray to God. They knew this was one law he would never follow.

Without thinking much about it, the king agreed.

Sure enough, the next day, Daniel did what he always did—he talked to God. He went to the rooftop of his house and prayed.

He thanked God for all the good things in his life. He asked God for help with the hard things.

Daniel knew about the new law, but he didn't want to hide his love for God. He refused to stop praying to God, no matter what the law said.

It was exactly what the other advisors had hoped.

The jealous advisors rushed to the king to tell him how Daniel had broken the new law. They insisted that he be punished by being thrown into a den full of hungry lions.

King Darius realized he had been tricked. He knew it wasn't really wrong for Daniel—or anyone—to talk to God.

The king tried to think of a way to save Daniel, but the law had already been signed. It couldn't be changed or broken.

So Daniel was arrested by the king's guards and hurled into the hungry lions' den.

As the soldiers rolled a large stone in front of the entrance to the cave, the sad-hearted king shouted to Daniel, "May God protect you!"

All night long, King Darius stayed awake
worrying about his friend, hoping and praying
that somehow he would be all right.

As soon as the sun came up, the king raced to the lions' den. He called, "Oh, Daniel, has your God been able to rescue you?"

He heard a voice reply, "Yes, my king! God sent an angel to shut the mouths of the lions! They haven't harmed me."

It was a miracle—Daniel was still alive!

Joy filled the king's heart. He told his guards to get Daniel from the lions' den immediately. Then he ordered that his evil advisors be thrown to the hungry lions instead.

The king couldn't wait to tell everyone in the kingdom the amazing story of how Daniel had honored God and God had saved him from the lions. King Darius and Daniel remained friends for the rest of their lives. And God continued to bless Daniel in every way.